Love:
The Greatest Command

Michael O Awotoye

WESTBOW
PRESS®
A DIVISION OF THOMAS NELSON
& ZONDERVAN

WestBow Press books may be ordered through
booksellers or by contacting:

WestBow Press
A Division of Thomas Nelson & Zondervan
1663 Liberty Drive
Bloomington, IN 47403
www.westbowpress.com
844-714-3454

Scripture quotations taken from The Holy Bible, New International
Version® NIV® Copyright © 1973 1978 1984 2011 by Biblica, Inc.
TM. Used by permission. All rights reserved worldwide.

ISBN: 978-1-6642-3253-2 (sc)
ISBN: 978-1-6642-3254-9 (e)

Library of Congress Control Number: 2021908495

Print information available on the last page.

WestBow Press rev. date: 5/14/2021

CONTENTS

CHAPTER 1

The Mystery of Love

There was once a hen that had just hatched her chick, and she was so happy to have someone else to love and take care of. The chick followed her mother everywhere she went. On one occasion, the hen saw some grains in a dirty but dry gutter and decided to feed her chick with those grains. She jumped into the gutter and the chick followed.

After feeding her chick, she flew out of the gutter only to realize that her precious chick could not follow. She went back into the gutter but was helpless. She strolled through the lengthy gutter hoping to find a way out for her chick, but she found none. She had no choice but to leave her lovely chick there. She went away and came back from time to time to check her chick, but that was not good enough. She could not bring any grains for her chick, nor could she shelter her chick for as long as she wanted. She became hopeless.

A passerby, seeing the helpless situation of the chick, decided to help. He brought a variety of grains and water for the chick to feed on at least three times a day and decided to continue this until the chick could fly out of the gutter. He also built a small tent to protect the chick, but each time he brought grains in the presence of the hen, the hen attacked him because she felt she could protect her chick. But definitely that did not stop him. Steadfastly, he continued bringing grains and water day after day.

I am sure you must be wondering why the man decided to nurture the chick. Could it be because he wanted to eat it after it matured? If so, does it mean the money and time he used to buy the grains for that long is more than what he would have used to buy one chicken in the market? Or could it be because he wanted the other hens to admire him? That does not make sense either.

The only obvious reason is that he loved the chicken, but why did he love that chick that much? Could it be because the man was jobless? If that was the case, had the man given up on his life much so that he never cared to pursue his interests? Why did he lavish the energy and resources he had on a hopeless chick? I guess the reason(s) is/are unexplainable, incomprehensible, and unsearchable.

Yet God, in the same manner, decided a long time ago to demonstrate this love. For years He had been declaring His love for His people through prophets from the time of Moses till the book of Malachi in the Bible, but the concept of His love was hard to comprehend. For us to understand better, He acted out of this love and gave His only Son to express and demonstrate how intense this love is "that while we were still sinners, Christ died for us" (Romans 5:7–8). He gave all by giving Jesus, just for us lowly humans, but why? Was it because of what we would do for Him after we recognized this great sacrifice? Not at all. According to Deuteronomy 7:7, He did this out of sheer love. What can we give in return? What can be likened to the love of God? Nothing can ever be compared with the great sacrifice made on that cross.

His love, unexplainable with words alone, had to be demonstrated. So He sent his Son to come and die so we could visually understand the extent of that love. But He did not stop there. He went a step further and sent his Spirit as a sign of our adoption into His family, to lead and guide us so that we will be just as He is, conformed to His image, and so that we too can express this love back to Him and unto our neighbors.

In testing whether Abraham loved Him or not, God told him to sacrifice his only son, Isaac (Genesis 22:1–18). He obeyed, and at the point of striking his son, God stopped him. Note that it was after Abraham demonstrated his love for God that God swore by Himself to bless Abraham, saying,

---

I swear by myself, declares the Lord, that because you have done this and not withheld your son, your only son, I will surely bless you and make your descendants as numerous as the stars in the sky and as the sand on the seashore. Your descendants will take possession of the cities of their enemies, and through your offspring, all nations on earth will be blessed, because you have obeyed me." Love is a mystery that once uncovered can provoke blessings from God. If you have love in you, then you have the right mindset to move on in life, and you will live enough for each day. Love makes us yearn to know more about how to be able to help others. Love is an expression of perfection.

CHAPTER 2

Mystery of Loving

Having love in you is a mystery, yet it is a virtue that no one wants to miss. Love is difficult to fathom, and mere words cannot define or express it properly, but it can only be manifested when it has made itself at home in you. The manifestation of love ranges from saying kind words to someone to making big sacrifices. God loves us, but more important is that God wants us to love others. He wants us to be expressions of His love, people who have experienced His love who in turn express this love to others. That is why, when asked what the greatest commandment was, Jesus replied,

> You must love the Lord your God with all your heart, all your soul, and all your mind. This is the first and greatest commandment. A second is equally important: Love your neighbor as yourself. (Matthew 22:36–39)

So it is important that in understanding that God loves us we reciprocate that love, but we go further and express this love to those around us, our neighbors.

This was also one of the reasons Jesus came to earth, aside from dying but also to lay down a pattern of love and sacrifice. Jesus loved His disciples deeply, even until the very end, and in the book of John, He exhorts His disciples to love each other in the same way He loved them. For it is in loving one another that they will prove to the world that they are truly His disciples (John 13:34–35). The same applies to us, for if we claim to be Christians (i.e., Christlike), the evidence for such a claim is that we love one another the way Christ loved us. But is it only fellow believers we are to love? What about the nonbelievers? Yes, they are included, for if we love only those who love us, if we love only those who are in our families, what reward is there? If we love only those who are capable of loving us, then our love has become conditional and is not in line with the pattern Christ laid for us because while we were yet sinners, before we loved Him or had Him in mind, He died for us.

This type of love, the one that loves without expecting anything back, is the type that transforms lives and leaves a lasting impact on the minds and hearts of people.

CHAPTER 3

What Love Is Not

A lot of people have different definitions of love. To firmly grasp the concept of love, it is important to first talk a little about what love is not, because when you know what something is not, you can better understand it and recognize it in whatever shape or form it is presented. This will tend to help you not to mistake something else for love.

Firstly, let us look at 1 Corinthians 13:1, which says, "If I speak in tongues of men and of angels, but have not love, I am only a resounding gong or a clanging cymbal." Regardless of how spiritual we might sound, whether in tongues of men or that of angels, if love does not reside within us, if love is not what motivates us to do what we do, we are only noisy bells. It tells us that speaking in tongues of men and of angels is not love. Do not get me wrong. I am not saying that speaking in tongues of men and of angels is wrong, but what we are looking out for here is the concept of love. So based on this concept, speaking in tongues is not exactly love; it could be an expression of love though. But love is a substance that must be present in your hearts for speaking in tongues to be effective.

Let's move ahead to the next verse, which says, "If I have the gift of prophecy and can fathom all mysteries and all knowledge, and if I have a faith that can move mountains, but have not love, I am nothing" (verse 2). Before I move further, it is important to note here that this verse categorically tells us that except love, all other virtues mentioned in that verse (like faith, knowledge, and the gift of prophecy) amount to nothing. This means that having love in you is very important in your life. Love is the starting point and the end of all virtues; it is the summation of all virtues. This point is important because many of us have broken down many times due to what we have experienced in the past or are experiencing now. In such experiences, many of us lose the meaning of love in our lives and go to different places trying only to establish faith, knowledge, and prophecies in our lives. But we have to understand that it is not enough to have faith that something good will happen in the future, it is not enough to accept that knowledge will change things, and prophesying about the future will not make better things come to pass.

It is all about your motive. Is it established in love or not?

Without love, faith just becomes an empty religious cycle and hope becomes an oxymoron because you cannot truly hope for something that you do not love. There is a fundamental need in life at all times to work toward God's perfect plan for us. That fundamental need is love. Having love in our lives is paramount if we must live happily.

Furthermore, the third verse says, "If I give all I possess to the poor and surrender my body to the flames, but have not love, I gain nothing." Of the three verses we have looked at so far in this chapter, this astonishes me the most. I have always thought that giving gifts to someone or receiving gifts from someone is love. But when I came across this verse,

I realized that there is something that must be added to giving for me to gain and be happy. That ingredient is love.

Giving should be brought forth from love. This means that aside from giving, there is something called love. It does not matter what you give; if there is no love in what you are sacrificing for your neighbor or God, it is nothing. Gifts are an expression of love but are not love in itself, so if you are giving a gift to someone to express a love that you do not have for them, you are deceiving yourself if you think it will be a substitute. It is not the gift that counts but the love behind it that matters most.

CHAPTER 4

Characteristics of Love

ow that you have seen a little bit of what love is not, let us talk about what love is. I must admit that this is a very tough topic that has been debated by a lot of people for centuries, but the Bible in many instances depicts what love is. Some of these are discussed here.

The first point I would like to discuss is that love has a personality just as God has. Love is like a person we have to admit to our lives. I am not talking about love from others; I am talking about love from God. Love is more than a word. It is embodied by a person: God! No one can give love, only God! We must first be admitted into love to have it. If we begin to understand that having love in our lives is a choice, we will go a long way in having it. It is good to realize that having love in our lives is our own choice and not the choice of any other person. It does not matter how a person has treated you or is treating you; you have a choice to be happy in love. This is particularly true if you love in God's way. The

Bible tells us that God demonstrated love to us even before we loved Him—that is, if we love Him at all. First John 4:8 ("because God is love") and 1 John 4:16 ("And so we know and rely on the love God has for us. God is love …") portray to us that God is love. He always earnestly waits for us to accept Him into us.

Secondly, love is whole and entire in nature; in fact, love is a nature. First Corinthians 13:9–12 says,

> For we know in parts and we prophesy in parts, but when perfection comes, the imperfect disappears. When I was a child, I talked like a child, I thought like a child, I reasoned like a child. When I became a man, I put childish ways behind me. Now we see but a poor reflection in a mirror; then we shall see face to face. Now I know in part; then I shall know fully, even as I am fully known.

Love is perfect for us. If we read the previous verses, from verse 4 to verse 8, the Bible describes love for us. It is worthy of note here that for love to exist in us, all those characteristics must be present. Look at those verses quickly.

> Love is patient, love is kind. It does not envy, it does not boast, it is not proud. It is not rude, it is not self-seeking, it is not easily angered, it keeps no record of wrongs. Love does not delight in evil but rejoices with the truth. It always protects, always trusts, always hopes, always perseveres. Love never fails.

All of these characteristics portray love. This implies that if we have patience and we are not kind, then love is not made perfect in us. It is just like saying you have hands but you do not have legs. I am not saying you should be looking out for all these characteristics in people. What I am saying is that you should be looking out for these (in their entirety) in yourself. You need to build up yourself in and through love if you want to be happy at all times and in every situation. Remember it is your responsibility to love. Love is whole and entire, and we must strive to attain this perfect will of God in our lives.

Also, love is an action word. In the Bible, God commanded us to love. Galatians 5:14 says, "The entire law is summed up in a single command: 'Love your neighbor as yourself.'" Obeying a command involves action. Loving others is something we have to do at every point in time. We are not supposed to love only when we feel or when we have feelings for others; love is not a feeling. But love is a fundamental that needs to be present even when we have feelings for a person or people. It is not every time we have feelings, yet we have to love all the time. It is not every person or situation we have feelings for, yet we have to love all the time. I am not saying you cannot find love in feelings.

I am saying that it is not in every feeling that you find love.

I perfectly understand that this concept of love as a personality, a fundamental, a nonnegotiable motivator for real life is and will be difficult for many to accept especially as it defies the dictionary meaning of love, but the better you accept this concept, the better you'll understand God's perfect will about loving.

Love is a doing word. We must decide to accept this command that we have been given. Loving is something we do consciously. In other words, we *decide* to love. We do not have to wait for a feeling and then unconsciously love. We have the ability to weigh the consequences of loving or not before we do so. But God expects us to always accept this command of love.

CHAPTER 5

So Why Not Love?

Love: The Greatest Command

The benefits of having love in us are so enormous. If I begin to talk about it, this book might never have an end. But I will just give you insight into what you can achieve if you have God's love in you.

If you have love in you, you will know God. He will live in you and others will know God through you. First John 4:7 says, "Dear friends, let us love one another, for love comes from God. Everyone who loves has been born of God and knows God." When I was much younger and started coming abreast with what life has to offer, I realized that there were three that were very difficult to understand and fathom for me: God, love, and life. But as I grew older, God began to open my eyes and unravel the true meaning of love to me. I realized that if anyone can understand the mystery of love, then that person has understood God and life.

God is love, and it is by loving that we can have a happy life.

> Yet for us there is but one God, the Father, from whom all things came and for whom we live; and there is but one Lord, Jesus Christ, through whom all things came and through whom we live.
>
> (1 Corinthians 8:6)

Friend, I tell you if you allow love in you, you are allowing God into you. And it is God you need to live your life. First Corinthians 8:3 says, "But the man who loves God is known by God." That is to say if you have love in you, you not only know God but you are known by God.

When Adam and Eve sinned, man lost contact with God. But now we have the means to get that contact back. That means is love. You can make the world the way God intended it to be for you. The only way is by having love in you.

Furthermore, if you have love in you, God will live in you and you will live in God. First John 4:12

says, "No one has ever seen God; but if we love one another, God lives in us, and his love is made complete in us." Little wonder God has always made a great emphasis on love. And it did not stop there. Verse 16 of that same chapter says, "And so we know and rely on the love God has for us. God is love. Whoever lives in love lives in God, and God in him." Those verses explain themselves.

Also, if you have love in you, you will have confidence. Ephesians 4:14–15 (emphasis mine) says,

> Then we will no longer be infants, tossed back and forth by the waves, and blown here and there by every wind of teaching and by the cunning and craftiness of men in their deceitful scheming. Instead speaking the truth in love, we will *in all things* grow up into him who is the Head, that is, Christ.

I italicized "in all things" so that I can make sure you do not miss it. Love gives us confidence in all things. I am sure you do not want to miss this grace for any reason.

Still talking about the confidence we have in love, 1 John 4:17 says, "In this way, love is made perfect among us so that we will have confidence on the day of judgment, because in this world we are like him." Well, I must confess I am not one of those who preach about the great tribulations that are to come (I don't undermine it though), but I believe if we focus on preaching love more, automatically the fear of the tribulations that are to come is overcome. Love in us will give us confidence. This leads us to the next point. If you have love, you will not be afraid. Take verse 18 of 1 John 4. "There is no fear in love. But perfect love drives out fear, because fear has to do with punishment. The one who fears is not made perfect in love." This is one of the reasons why the law did not work. Each time we try to follow the law, we remind ourselves of our sins. For example, if you are a chronic fornicator and somebody comes to you and all he keeps saying is that you should not fornicate, he only keeps reminding you about fornication. The question is "How do you stop fornicating when you have the nature of fornication?" You must renew your mind by constantly thinking and meditating on the right things. The right thing you should be thinking about in this context is not "Do not fornicate" but things like "My body is the temple of the Holy Spirit." I tell you, if you truly love God and you imbibe and follow the teaching that your body is the temple of the Holy Spirit, you will not fornicate. You need to have the nature of God to stop fornicating.

When you have God's love in you, you fulfill the law.

Let no debt remain outstanding, except the continuing debt to love one another, for he who loves his fellowman has

> fulfilled the law. The commandments, "Do not commit adultery," "Do not murder," "Do not steal," "Do not covet," and whatever other commandments there may be, are summed up in this one rule: "Love your neighbor as yourself." (Romans 13:8–9)

That is another huge topic I'm not going into in this book. But we will see a little more about renewing your mind in the next chapter.

Now when you have love in you, you have the stature of God. Ephesians 3:19 says, "And to know this love that surpasses knowledge—that you may be filled to the measure of the fullness of God." The Bible says in Psalm 82:6 that you are gods. If love is made perfect in you, you will be like God Himself.

So why should you love?

Because there is power in love.

First Corinthians 4:20–21 says,

For the kingdom of God is not a matter of talk but of power. What do you prefer? Shall I come to you with a whip, or in love and with a gentle spirit?

Love has the following power:

- power of doing the right things
- power of changing things and situations
- power of building up
- power of living and not just existing
- power of overcoming
- power of restoration

The list is endless.

CHAPTER 6

Making the Love
of God Yours

*L*oving is a choice. The first step in having God's love in you is to desire to love God and your neighbor. I do not know what burden you are carrying in your heart and your mind. You might have been hurt due to broken relationships or betrayal of trust. I do not know how bad the situation is looking. But what I do know is that God can heal and touch you in and through love. You need to choose to commune with God in love. God is calling on you and knocking at the door of your heart today. You need to open your heart and mind to him. You need to accept His love. His love is perfect for you at all times and in all situations.

I believe you've made that choice now. Don't stop there. Pray that God will perfect His love in you. Ephesians 3:17–19 says,

> And I pray that you, being rooted and established in love, may have power, together with all the saints, to grasp how wide and long and high and deep is the

> love of Christ, and to know this love that surpasses knowledge—that you may be filled to the measure of the fullness of God.

You can take a little while now to stop reading and pray. Pray that God should open your eyes to see and recognize His love for you. Tell Him that you are ready to walk in His love and that He should teach you how.

Now I am continuing this book believing that you have made a choice to love and that you have prayed to God. It is time to start renewing your mind. Romans 12:2 says, "Do not conform any longer to the pattern of this world, but be transformed by the renewing of your mind. Then you will be able to test and approve what God's will is—his good, pleasing, and perfect will." Renewing your mind is a continual thing. It involves constantly filling your mind with the right things.

Philippians 4:8 says, "Finally, brothers, whatever is true, whatever is noble, whatever is right, whatever is pure, whatever is lovely, whatever is admirable—if anything is excellent or praiseworthy—think about such things." Let me give you an analogy about renewing your mind. Consider a cup filled with dirty water. If you continue to pour clean water into it so that the water overflows from the cup, the water that will be in the cup will become cleaner and cleaner until it eventually becomes perfectly clean.

I do not know how dirty your heart is right now, but I tell you it can become clean. Give God a chance. Give love a chance. John 14:23 says, "Jesus replied, 'If anyone loves me, he will obey my teaching. My Father will love him, and we will come to him and make our home with him.'" That's a big opportunity God is offering you. Maybe you don't understand. Let me explain. The God who made heaven and earth wants to come, together with His power and splendor, into your heart, mind, and life so that you too can create just as He creates. Only if you will love God and your neighbor. "Love must be sincere. Hate what is evil; cling to what is good"

(Romans 12:9). "Do not be overcome by evil, but overcome evil with good" (Romans 12:21).

Finally, you must take action. You have to start loving God and loving your neighbor. Put what you are learning from God into action. When you take action, you are manifesting that love in you. It is in taking action that you actually do God's command of loving.

Matthew 25 tells us of the parable of the sheep and goats. In verses 35 and 36, Jesus was saying,

> For I was hungry and you gave me something to eat, I was thirsty and you gave me something to drink, I was a stranger and you invited me in, I needed clothes and you clothed me, I was sick and you looked after me, I was in prison and you came to visit me.

Then verse 40 says, "I tell you the truth, whatever you did for one of the least of these brothers of mine, you did for me."

Printed in the United States
by Baker & Taylor Publisher Services